Goods and Services Around Town

Heather E. Schwartz

Consultants

Shelley Scudder
Gifted Education Teacher
Broward County Schools

Caryn Williams, M.S.Ed.
Madison County Schools
Huntsville, AL

Publishing Credits

Dona Herweck Rice, *Editor-in-Chief*
Lee Aucoin, *Creative Director*
Torrey Maloof, *Editor*
Diana Kenney, M.A.Ed., NBCT,
   Associate Education Editor
Marissa Rodriguez, *Designer*
Stephanie Reid, *Photo Editor*
Rachelle Cracchiolo, M.S.Ed., Publisher

Image Credits: Cover & pp. 1, 19 Alamy; pp. 13, 16, 17 Getty Images; pp. 3, 15 iStockphoto; pp. 20, 21 (top) Jamey Acosta; p. 21 Jaden Acosta and Bailee Faddoul; p. 6 The Library of Congress [LC-D4-43107]; p. 8 The Library of Congress [LC-USF34-082538]; p. 10 The Library of Congress [LC-USZ62-41874]; p. 12 The Library of Congress [LC-USZ62-118145]; p. 14 The Library of Congress [LC-USZ62-17117]; All other images from Shutterstock.

Teacher Created Materials

5301 Oceanus Drive
Huntington Beach, CA 92649-1030
http://www.tcmpub.com

ISBN 978-1-4333-6978-0
© 2014 Teacher Created Materials, Inc.

Table of Contents

For Sale

What can you buy in your town? Look around you. There are many **goods** and **services** (SUR-vis-iz) to buy.

This boy buys a snow cone on a hot day.

This girl shovels snow on a cold day.

Good Stuff

Goods are things that you can buy. Books are goods. Computers are goods, too.

A woman shops at a bookstore long ago.

This girl is shopping for a book today.

At Your Service

Services are work or help that is for sale. Fixing a car is a service. Cleaning a home is a service, too.

A man is paid to fix a car long ago.

This woman is paid to fix a car today.

Make It, Sell It, or Buy It

Producers (pruh-DOO-serz) make goods. **Sellers** sell the goods. **Consumers**, or buyers, shop for goods and services.

This woman makes shoes long ago.

Buy It!

Buyers can also be called *customers* or *clients*. They can be called *guests* or *shoppers*, too.

These customers are buying flowers.

11

Producers choose what to make. They make goods that buyers **want** and **need**.

These men are making cars long ago.

These women are making baseball gloves today.

Sellers choose what to sell. They decide the **prices**. They sell goods and services at prices people will pay.

This store has a sale on toys long ago.

Low Prices!

Some sellers sell the same goods as others. They lower their prices so buyers will buy from them.

This store has lots of things on sale today.

Buyers choose which goods and services they want to buy. They choose the prices they will pay.

Many people want to buy dolls in 1983.

I Want It!

If buyers all want the same goods, then sellers will raise their prices.

These people are in line to buy the latest cell phone.

Your Town

Your town has producers and sellers. They work together so you can buy what you want and need.

This dad is buying his son new shoes.

Do I Need That?

Some things you want. Other things you need. You may *want* a new toy. But you *need* food.

This girl wants to buy a toy.

Make It!

Are you good at reading? Do you like to clean your room? Think of a way you can help people. You may help friends with homework. You may help them clean. Make a poster to tell people about your service.

Bailee and Jaden love dogs.

Jaden and Bailee make a poster to tell about their dogsitting business.

Little Ones Dog Sitters
Big or small, we ♥ them all!
Only $5.00 per hour

.Walking   . loving

.feeding   . playing

          Call Us
Jaden & Bailee

Glossary

consumers—people who buy things

goods—things people can buy

need—to know you must have something

prices—amounts of money needed to
  buy things

producers—people who make things

sellers—people who sell things

services—work or help for sale

want—to feel you would like to have
  something but do not need it

Index

Your Turn!

Find the Goods

This boy is getting new shoes. Shoes are goods. Look around your classroom or house. What goods can you find? Make a list.